# Rebel Moon

# Rebel Moon

## @narchist
## rants & poems

### Norman Nawrocki

Edinburgh • London
San Francisco

Rebel Moon
ISBN #1 873176 08 2

AK PRESS    AK PRESS
P.O. Box 40682   P.O. Box 12766
San Francisco,CA   Edinburgh, Scotland
94140-0682 USA   EH89YE


Library of Congress Cataloging in Publication Data:

A catalogue record for this title is available from the Library of
Congress.


British Library Cataloguing in Publication Data:

A catalogue record for this title is available from the British Library.

Graphics:   Dave Lester
Back cover photo:   Lincoln Clarkes
Photo page 41:   Carla Nemiroff
Photo page 91:   Claude Majeau

Cover design: a.h.s. boy, Dada Typographics — Baltimore
Book design: katiemur, Dada Typographics — Montréal

Printed & bound in the USA

For Irene & Frank Nawrocki

# CONTENTS

# PREFACE

Few of the pieces in this collection were ever conceived as quiet ink for a calm page. Most came kicking and screaming demanding a life of their own beyond paper. So I took them to the stage as spoken word material, each with their own distinct voice, sometimes with or without music. But as friends once told me early on when they first heard my work live: "Well, it's not quite poetry, nor is it really song or theatre. It's a mix. It has rhythm. It deals with social issues. It's activist. It's more like 'rhythm activism'."

Thus, "rhythm activism" summed up best what I did with my alley poems, news poems, garbage can poems, agit-prop pieces and odd chunks of cabaret whenever I performed.

More than a style, "Rhythm Activism" became the name of a poetry/music ensemble that eventually grew into a full scale "rebel news orchestra," a "rock 'n roll cabaret," known for its "electrified alternative journalism" and high energy theatrical performances. Many of the pieces in *Rebel Moon* can actually be heard with music on the band's CD and cassette recordings. Others come from my assorted one-man cabaret shows and readings.

For the purposes of this volume, much of the material has been edited for the printed page. Refrains have disappeared. Facial expressions cut. Costumes and assorted theatrics nixed.

Keep in mind, too, there are rants and poems here that were written for use in the street, for soup lines and picket lines, for demonstrations and public awareness campaigns, not only to entertain, but to help inform, organize and ultimately, empower. This was and always will be the inspiration for much of my writing.

For your own pleasure, try reading this book out loud, with and without your own music. Make it an interactive read. And don't hesitate to talk up "the Idea" contained within. These are words to be recycled in everyday battles for freedom, justice and dignity, as much in the kitchen and bedroom as on the street or at work.

And if, in passing, some of them can bring a smile to a tired face, good.

Norman Nawrocki
Montréal, 1996

# RATS

We're the rats your Mama warned you about
We're coming out of the sewers
We're alive under your feet
We crawl on all fours
We scrounge garbage cans
We live in the dark
We bite, bellies empty
lean looks our fashion
baggy clothes our disguise

We're the rats you never see
We see you
We gnaw on nothing
whetting our appetites
for well–fed men and women
their footsteps heavy
under diamonds and mink
We hear spare change rustling
loose in their boardrooms
drinking champagne they clink

Have you hugged a rat today?
Have you fed a rat today?
We're the rats poking pink noses
out of manholes and closets
and holes in the windows
that let in the cold

We're the rats squealing crazy
You don't hear us
We hear you
We hide in dark corners
We flash no smiles
just teeth

sharpened on nothingness
the largesse you dare to offer
We bite for less

Winter and summer
the sewers stink
turn you blind
run red with rat blood
thousands of bodies
floating in circles
slowly
There's no race down here
just rotting leftovers
hard to avoid
flushed clean past our faces
Rats smell
unless you never noticed

Have you screwed a rat today?
Pick us up cheap right downtown
In the cover of night
we're cute even desirable
flushed hot with hunger
we'll squirm under your sheets
You call the tune

And you call this
the Year of the Rat?
We puke
You want primmed, perfumed
model rats
the ugliest of us all, that's right
clawing their way
to the rat heap top

standing proud
on just two legs
straining to breathe
fresh air and your turds
Come the Year of the Rat Revolt
they'll hang
by their tails
squealing for you

Train us to say "cheese"
will you
Train us to chase our tails
will you
Train us to push the right buttons
and we'll blow you to hell
Rat Heaven on Earth come true

We're the rats
your Mama warned you about
Smell us strong
through your plate–glass windows
Your laws we defy them
Your gods we deny them
We honour no king
We march ragged for none
but ourselves

The pack our column
The night our day
The wind knows we're near

Trap us one by one
our necks will snap with ease
Catch us thousands strong

if you dare
You'll never sleep again
We guarantee
There's no cage big enough
for all the rats of this world
No hole deep enough
to bury us all alive
No oven hot enough
to annihilate us
If you tried
our blackened noses
could sniff you out
wherever you might hide

so watch it

We're the rats
your Mama warned you about
We're coming
out of the sewers

# JOHN CLARKE

By 6am
the first Monday
of every month
John Clarke,
an 82 year old diabetic
walks 6 blocks
to the bus stop,
catches 3 buses,
waits in line
for 3 hours
for the Food Bank handout of
a loaf of bread,
a tray of biscuits,
peanut butter,
canned corn,
peas and beans,
instant pudding,
and a few apples and oranges
"Luckily I know how to get by"
he says
"But it's awful rough
for a lot of old people"

# AFTERNOON RAG

Somebody's mother
unwound the grand clock
and it's hissing spoiled wine
all over the carpet

the shoeshine man's
rubbing out the fear
poking through your soles
a dollar for your trouble

the neighbour's monkey
is riding Shirley's back
digging into her arm
carving another track

while the stairs
suffer bills
a calculated crime
'cause the headlines say it all
Remember Who's Mine?

Hey brother George
can you spare me a swig
before the moon falls down
and the Captain muffs his jig

someone's cackling
at the seat of my pants
where roaches sometimes gather
to toast the King of France

see the rain lickin' my face
it's the worst bitter brew
can't wash away the years
of tears staining my crutch

But hey brother George
can you spare me a swig
'cause the ache in my heart
is gonna knock me dead
before the mailman ever
knocks again

that skipper and his rope
gotta last another round
'cause the fight never begins
on the other side of town
before the lady's ready
to hire an extra clown

do you think
we'll ever see her
500 metres tall
if she swings her arms
and attacks a shopping mall

can the voice of unreason
reduce the waiting time
if the saviour never found her
will the circus remind her

is the statue of liberty
insured for its fall
watch the roosters
crowing my way
leading milkmen to the door
watch sharpshooters breathing
softly beneath the neon floor
maybe the scarecrow carving
will set an extra plate

for the devil's apple pie
tattooed underground

no I never smoked alone
in the jungles of China
I never cleaned my teeth
with a piece of her mind
I only took the picture
when the gully fell away

So hey brother George
can you spare me a swig
I think I'm gonna plug
the corner over there

# BUNGLED UP B & E

Hey guys, you blew it
you can't rip off
13 cases of beer
2 boxes of brandy
and a dozen bottles
of fine red Portuguese wine
early Sunday morning
through a back door
off the alley
and expect you're gonna
make clean your getaway
when every local is
already washing up
for Jesus

No way, man, it's group hari–kari
silly business from too much late night TV
no gang of 12 year olds
running down a quiet residential street
at seven in the morning
each with two cases of beer under their arms
is gonna convince someone's mother
it's all for the 9 o'clock mass
'round the corner

When will you learn
they'll get you nearly every time
'cause you're just chicken feed,
throwaway youth,
poor East End kids without a future
who keep the cops' pay cheques coming
you're part of the local employment scene, guys,
but the difference is,
you never get yours

you end up in reform school
behind bars in doctor's notebooks
on social workers caseloads in little computers
everywhere
with just another story to tell
all for a few bucks and warm beer
you'd piss away anyway

No, kids,
you weren't cool
you woke me and all the sleeping dogs on the block
that's no way to do a B & E
the morning peace went
when you started to fuck up so loudly
Nothing was on your side
except a popout aluminum window frame
and a grey alley going nowhere

So when you gonna learn
little brothers and sisters
you've got to find a way they can't touch you
you've got to use those supple limbs
and nimble minds and all your guts
together
to break out of – not into
the mess we left you

then smash it to bits
melt down all the chains
and start all over again
you can do it
you can do it
and the beer
will taste better

# REDIRECTING THE IONS

A naked magician
wanders muddied fields
of urban splendour
trailing webs of compassion
for the lowliest unseen

He reassembles buildings
presses trees and flowers
through high–pitched cracks
shivering chords of ecstasy

He unwedges parked cars
melts them down into
singing, flying chimes
of recycled melody
eternally airborn
playgrounds of glitter
flashing in the wind

He beckons roots unholy
to crawl out from the dark
twisting and chanting
skyward
in harmony
without remorse

He pirouettes amazed
on green glass slippers
delirious beneath the enchanted symphony
stroking his beard of
crushed grey tears
wondering why
the misery
can still be heard

# THE BLACK FLAG

Hello! Are you bothered by sleepless nights,
Yuppies gnawing away at your neighbourhood?
Do you suffer from nightmares about being roasted alive at
a Yuppie barbecue?
Do you go bananas when you hear Yuppies gnashing their
BMW gearboxes or popping champagne corks
to toast new condominiums on your block?
If so, then you've got a problem
and you need a proven Yuppie pest control:

THE BLACK FLAG

Comes with a heavy–duty, no nonsense, stainless steel
flag pole
good for 100 Yuppie exterminations.

THE BLACK FLAG

when used properly,
will unleash unruly punk rockers, riff raff, condo evictims,
old age pensioners and general malcontents
and provoke immediate panic in any nest of Yuppies.

Plant it on a Yuppie lawn and you can
raise hell 'til the break of dawn;
Plant it through their tinted windshields
and watch their smiles crumble;
Plant it through the tips of their Gucci shoes
and hear them holler (ha! ha!);
Plant it through the front door of their condos
and watch them scurry away and hide.

THE BLACK FLAG

The people's choice. Used for centuries by leading
professionals everywhere,

from the Paris Commune to the streets of
Chicago and L.A.
Works where other pest controls fail.
It's odourless, too, and will not destroy the ozone.

DON'T LET A DIM-WITTED YUPPIE
MAKE YOUR LIFE MISERABLE.

Fight back.
Use THE BLACK FLAG, and shove it up their
brand name Yuppie ass.
Comes with a smart, two-tone vinyl carrying case.
Don't be the last on your block to fly one.
Get yours today.

# A BUCK A BODY

*Based on a true story about a man on Death Row in a Texas prison.*

And the Angels of Death visited prisoner Robert S.
condemned to die, because he robbed, and killed for a dollar,
oh my

"So you ran out of luck buddy,
chasing a lousy buck
If you'd prayed to us sooner, we could have tipped you off
to a winner, 'cause

*A buck a body is no way to get rich*
*But dig a hole deep enough*
*and you'll bury the itch*

"Let's say you could have prayed for a factory
to mass produce misery,
maiming and polluting at will, your own license to kill
We could have blessed your enterprise
showered you with holy water,
made you rich and famous, a proud father with sons
and daughter
You could have stood tall in the community
Mr. Respectable, given to charity
and if anyone noticed the crimes of your factory
shrugged it off with a business morality, 'cause

*A buck a body is no way to get rich*
*Dig a hole deep enough*
*You'll bury that itch*

And the Angels of Death looked prisoner Robert S. straight
in the eye and sighed

"What a pity, why?
You know you could have prayed
for a seat in government, been courted by hawks for peace
voted to outfit killer armies to protect the pure
and slaughter the diseased
No one would question the connection,
ask the amount of your cut
You'd be defending "freedom"
and the right to make your buck, 'cause

> *A buck a body is no way to get rich*
> *But dig a hole deep enough*
> *and you bury that itch*

"You could have lobbied with whiskey
to make the death penalty the law
for any poor sucker who tried to do it his own way
Then on the day the news broke, about a dollar hiest,
a dollar stiff, we'd have propped you up
frothing and blue, to denounce the crime
and the shocking motive, too
Instead, you poor bugger,
It's You who's gonna die
A needle up the arm, no one's gonna cry, 'cause

> *A buck a body was no way to get rich*
> *But if you'd dug a hole deep enough*
> *You could have buried that itch*

And prisoner Robert S.
listened to the Angels of Death
and shaking his head, twitching after the injection,
he muttered under his last breath:

"A buck a body, it's no way to get rich
So dig me a hole deep enough and bury me beside
someone already rich
I want to borrow their suit and come back dressed to kill
Then I can gouge the innocent, gouge the poor
and pay your bill, 'cause

> *A buck a body is no way to get rich*
> *You've got to dig a hole deep enough*
> *You've got to bury that itch*

And the Angels of Death
left prisoner Robert S.
alone to die
because he robbed and he killed for a dollar,
                              oh my

# CINDY LIVES THE GOOD LIFE

Cindy couldn't make it
for the free food today
little Lou, Ricky and the baby
cried the door shut

Can't blame the kids
besides
who's got money for the bus
there's no sitter
it really isn't worth that much trouble
the stroller needs fixing
and anyway
the bus ride is as long as the lineup
at that "bank" or longer
because the transfers
never make it on time or wait
for a single mother
with three bawling children
and just two hands

So what's a lost bag of jello,
pork and beans, Kraft dinner,
a few carrots, potatoes, bread,
cookies and sliced ham, maybe

This week's dinner?

# GONNA FEED 36

Gonna walk into that big food store
Gonna take three dozen friends or more
Gonna load our buggys full of grub
Gonna munch our way up and down the floor

Gonna wiggle our bums to the looney tunes
Gonna toss in the stuff fill the buggys real soon
Gonna push them through the cashier stall
Gonna say: "It's OK friend, the food's on them!"

Gonna wheel right out the swinging door
36 buggys full — maybe more
When people start asking: "What'd you do that for?"
Gonna say: "What'd ya think, it's a People's War!"

Gonna eat real well so we can do it some more
Gonna pass 'round the wealth from the big food store
36 friends strong — maybe some more
Gonna feed ourselves like never before

# GALVANIZED

Me?
I've been
renovated
upgraded
condomized
gentrified
relocated
vacated
upscaled
displaced
remodelled
expropriated
privatized
terrorized
dispossessed
repossessed
evicted
restricted
and kicked right out

Now
I've been thinking
and drinking
crying and
whining
trying real hard
to figure it all out
I've been reading
and writing
talking and
squawking
asking why
it's always me

that's gotta go
So now me
and my neighbours
are all hooting
and hollering
refusing to move
barricading doors
and all the windows too

'cause we're contesting
protesting
defying
resisting
organized
persisting
pissed off
fighting mad
and tired of getting
relocated
vacated
upscaled
displaced
evicted
restricted
and kicked right out
This time,
we're staying

# HARD TIMES

When the sun can't melt
the ice coating our bones
nor thaw the blood
clogging our veins
We pace
We pace the city — your city, it's not ours
We don't call it "proud"

We walk the distance between here
and tomorrow — it's your future — not ours
We walk in the shadows of your corporate glory
We slip and slide down your
tried and tiring ways
We cross streets named in your honour,
for your saints and heros — not ours
We step on the cracks cursing
your grand plans
We circle monumental blocks of monied shops
the obscene repositories of your hoarded wealth
We flip through your twisted journals and read the news
and we mark these times as Hard Times and
Hard Times are your times — not ours

We're the ragged the haggard the worn and weary
the sallow–skinned faces eyes bloodshot and bleary
We're the bawling the bleeding open sores leaking
the shadows in your dark the denizens of the car park
You file us away on sagging shelves til we fall off with
a crash and a scream for justice

We're the forgotten the forsaken
the one–in–five barely alive the scavengers in front of you
on a Friday night
We're the upright drowsers toothless smilers blood salesmen

guinea pigs you play with
Pain? What pain? Colour us blind we're still on your screen
you can't zap us away
We're the howling broken pieces spit out of your machine
the rejects rejectable margins of acceptable loss
We're your canned TV laughter hysterical out of control
weeping bloody tears you'd never know

"You recognize me, Sir? Spare a dollar, Sir? Spare a job?
Wanna blow job?"

We're last night's garbage recycled each hour
We crawled out of the pit where you left us
faceless nameless creditcardless you couldn't care less
We're expendable forgettable victims of your excess
and we're fucking tired of these times
'cause these times are Hard Times and they're your times —
     not ours

Listen!
     Our times are buzzin' round our brains
     like mad bumblebees
     Our times are fistfuls of exploding stars
     clenched in your face
     Our times are ticking softly under your pillow
     within our reach
     'cause our times are Rebel Times and
     they're always 'round the corner

When we can spit out the fire burning in our bellies
When we can rip out the bricks you laid over our bones and
heave them through your windows your homes
When we can crack the codes that bind us
to a numbing blindness

34

When we can slice through your walls of fear and deceit
like a hot knife straight from hell
When we can roll back your barbed wire with our bare hands
and haul each other across your wasteland to the mountains
beyond
When we can overturn your Jags, Rolls and limos
and set them smoking in the midnight sun
When we can talk straight loud and clear with nothing to lose
When we can count angry hands razor minds and raging spirits
                    all together
       your city will be ours and our times will begin
       Our Times — a city where misery knows no home
                    where hunger knows no belly
                    where shame knows no soul
                    where our wildest dreams are your nightmare
Until then
We pace the city — your city
We don't call it "proud"

# FLORENCE

*A retired 79 year old waitress, waiting in line at the Food Bank, said:*
*"There are funeral expenses to worry about,*
*I have to save some money for that and take care of myself."*

When I die
I'm gonna bury myself
I've got no family
There is no one else

I've used my life savings
to buy a cemetery plot
Even bought a headstone
sure cost a lot

The coffin's another story
I still need a grand
When you're a retired waitress
you save what you can

I won't have anything left
to pay no preacher man
I'm gonna do it all myself
You betcha I can

I'll dig the hole
I already have a shovel
I'll push the coffin in
won't be any trouble
I'll say a few words
make the sign of the cross
I'll shed no tears for myself
I'm no loss

I'll step in with dignity
and close the lid
Figure if I move around enough
that fresh—smelling, loose earth will just fall in

I'll leave the rest
to the wind and the rain
they'll finish the job
even write my name:

"Here lies a woman who could take care
of herself
From birth to death
she never relied on anyone else"

# JACK DAW

Jack Daw clawed his way from the grave
the man who took his land
no preacher could save
13 miles on a gravel road
he crawled on his belly
he crawled on his nose

> "Oh Lord forgive me and rest my soul
> I'm a dead man cursed with what I know
> I died in my sleep but the man who killed me
> keeps hurtin' others and still goes free"

That man was the agent
from the big bank in town
foreclosing farms for miles around
killing poor farmers stealing their dreams
Crimes of the banker heartless and mean

Jack Daw clawed his way from the grave
his heart wasn't beating but he was enraged
His eyes glowed white a ghastly sight
this dead man crawling
in the pale moon light

He reached the bank for opening time
Folks shrieked and fled he was first in line
A dead man crawling no banker'd ever seen
burst into his office cursing and mean

> "I've come a long way to claim what's mine
> I'm back from the dead I hope you don't mind
> You killed me so you could balance your books
> Now I'm here to balance mine
> Take a good look!"

With a crooked bony hand
Jack yanked him to the floor
then dragged the screaming banker out the door
He didn't struggle long they say he died of fright
And old Jack Daw dragged him out of sight

Later they shut that cursed bank down
'cause every new banker
vanished from town
not a trace was left nothing could be found
But everyone knew
Yes everyone knew
Old Jack Daw had been around

# SQUAT THE CITY!

SQUAT the City! FUCK the rent!
PAY no landlord! PAY no rent!

When that knock comes on the door
The monthly ransom's due once more
Do you pay? Do you squawk?

SQUAT the City! FUCK the rent!
PAY no landlord! PAY no rent!

Who built the place you call your home?
Hammered the nails and laid the stone?
Who makes big bucks off others' work?
Collects the rent and stuffs his shirt?

Rent the roaches — what a deal!
He won't charge extra — he's no heel!
Crunch them in your cornflakes bowl
Stuff them in that gaping hole
why don't we

SQUAT the City! FUCK the rent!
PAY no landlord! PAY no rent!

Twist his arm you need some heat
Twist his leg your stairs eat feet
On knee no cap a smile a wink
Beg my lord please fix the sink

Pennies fall it's a welfare cheque
They roll into your landlord's pocket
Will you eat? The cupboard's bare
Watch him buy another gold locket
why don't we

SQUAT the City! FUCK the rent!
PAY no landlord! PAY no rent!

Eviction notice time to move
Same old story now you're screwed
Pack your bags and move your ass
Add your name to the homeless mass

Tramp those streets a merry–go–round
Search for a place none are sound
Find one move in repair that floor
Ouch! A rent hike! You know the score

SQUAT the City! FUCK the rent!
PAY no landlord! PAY no rent!

Speculators mortgage takers
Bank those bucks we pay for housing
Bank of Commerce, American Savings
Montrea – a – a – a – a – a – a –

All they do is mark up property
Steal your rent they're making money!
Holy fakers leeches robbers undertakers
Let's get smart

SQUAT the City! FUCK the rent!
PAY no landlord! PAY no rent!

People in chains were masters' folk
But slaves those chains they finally broke
Now we're slaves to the working day
Slaving on 'cause there's rent to pay

Half our income down the drain
Pay for shelter? It's a pain
Tenants are *feudal*, landlords too
Time to rebel time for us to

SQUAT the City! FUCK the rent!
PAY no landlord! PAY no rent!

# ALL MY LIFE

I lived with a woman
who came home one night and told me
she'd been harassed by two men in the street
I asked her
"Why didn't you say something, fight back,
put them in their place?"
and she looked me in the eyes and said:
 "All my life
  I've had to put up with men in the street
  total strangers who think they're God's gift
  to women
  they've
  pawed at me
  grabbed me
  brushed against me
  stared at me
  leered at me
  bumped into me
  tried to cop a feel from me
  stroked my hair
  twisted it in their hands
  whistled at me
  followed me
  blocked me
  screamed at me
  ridiculed me
  terrorized me
  insulted me
  stood in front of me
  went out of their way to
  brush against me
  laughed at me
  tested me

rolled their windows down
and yelled at me
demanded my name and number
saying they wanted to
get to know me
asked me to
suck them, fuck them, marry them
in the street
All my life
All my life
and I'm used to it
and that's the way it goes
If I took time out each day, each night
to deal with it on the spot
I wouldn't have a life
I'd be doing nothing else"
And I looked into her eyes
and I didn't know what to say
And all I could feel was the sickness
in my stomach
And all I could do
was write this down and tell you
tell all men
that this
has got to stop

# DINK THINK

hot heavy date
he won't be late
shines his shoes
forgets the blues
checks for the safes
no taking chances
it's cracker night
another deposit box
he knows his trade
can pick all the locks
so he picks her up
and away they go

she's aglow she's on fire
he's a drinker he won't tire
music catches heart beat cock beat
    "hear my drums beat love like a dove
      on the weenie weenie warpath"
they fall for cologne the fancy dinner
the club scene's extra
it goes with dessert
at $10 a squirt it can't hurt huh
he's no jerk

    this honey thinks I'm funny
    she's laughing on my shoulder
    knows who spends the money
    he's in control here
    time to lead her on to our moonlit future
    "your place or mine?"

    turn the lights real low
    "relax and come closer"
    "you don't want to fool around?"

"I'm no imposer"
"come a little closer"
"come a little closer"

close her lips seal them with honey
relax her thighs pet the lovely bunny
kiss her palms soothe her qualms
silence her alarms 'cause lover boy's here

soft like ice cream fresh breath mint clean
the guy won't fight
it's date rape tonight
he knows her number and he makes his move

objections over–ruled
guess who's on top
objections over–ruled
guess who won't stop
objections over–ruled
    "there's nothing to fear"
    "let's do it right here"
    "I got protection"
    "open wider"
objections over–ruled
lover boy's here and he's into the box

smooth like whipped cream slippery hands unseen
the guy won't fight
it's date rape tonight
"if we're friends and I really do like you
it's gotta be alright, right?"
it's alright tonight, right? ugh
it's alright tonight, right? ugh
"hey what's the matter don't you like it?"
ugh ugh ugh

# A LONG RIDE ON THE BUS

I'm riding the bus late at night
young woman gets on sits alone on the right
older man gets on sits on the other side
he starts staring at her, like really staring at her
Here comes a long ride, a really long ride
on the bus

She fidgets and turns, moves closer to the window
He crosses the aisle faces her resting on his elbow
now he's leering at her, like really leering at her
Here comes a long ride, a really long ride
on the bus

He doesn't take his eyes off her I can't take mine off him
What to do?
can't ignore him late at night on the bus
the driver, him, her and me just the four of us
I could say:
         "Hey dude quit staring at her"
I could say:
         "Driver this guy's bugging her do something"
What do I say to her?

So I move closer to him and say quite clearly
         "Hey buddy you got the time I don't want to miss the Simpson's
that guy Homer he just cracks me up he's better than hockey and I'm
a Canadian's fan myself how about you I like to watch the games
with a monster bag of chips and tons of chocolate ice cream
and loads of beer and onion rings it really passes the time I'm
unemployed how about you I can watch TV for hours there are so
many cool shows on like..." and before anyone knows it she's off the
bus and the guy's looking at me like what the but I don't stop 'cause I
like to talkand it's a long ride, a really long ride — for him —
on the bus

# MORE THAN A WAX & SHINE

Hey dude! You tired of being called a "dickhead?" Tired of being a slave to your wee wee? Come on down to "Crazy Nat's Car Wash & Penile Lobotomy Centre" and we'll take care of you and yours!

In the time it takes to wash and wax your car, we'll get rid of that pesky, bothersome pea–sized brain in your penis and turn you into a new man!

Just think! Now, you can be in charge of your sexual desires and your hard ons! It's easy!

At "Crazy Nat's" we use the latest laser surgery to give you a painless, one shot penile lobotomy. No mess! No fuss! So do yourself a favour! Get rid of those embarrassing "mind of it's own" erections — the ones you know you can live without! Remove the "dick–tator" from your dick! Ha! Ha! Put yourself back in the driver's seat!

And we guarantee you'll pee straighter!

# COUPLES: A STUDY

Couples couple!
They couple in the shadows, drive—ins,
restaurants and laundry room
They walk each other in the park holding hands
Hands holding the couple
New couples cut cake exactly in half
Older couples buy a house, practice the rhythm method and
hide the cake
from each other
Old couples love to counsel newer couples
Some couples multiply or play game shows and win
A winning couple, how can they lose
A trouble—free ain't life wonderful couple
made for each other
A perfect fit under the covers couple stuck together
unable to separate

Coupled and still living, Coupled and still wondering,
Coupled to keep fit, Coupled to keep each other
Keep on coupling and become a model couple
just like in the re—runs
Couple for peace of mind, Couple for a piece of the action
At night couples pair off and make whoopee
During the day couples separate and shout
"Whoopee!"

Strangers often pass couples in the street
like last month's couple, this week's couple, the five years and
still going couple,
the long—distance feeling couple,
the significant other couple,
the not quite but almost there couple

Jogging couples, flogging couples, groggy couples, a
"we–just–broke–up–and–got–back–together couple"
A couple of survivors narrowly avoiding a "couple buster"
you know the type:
a coupable third person
looking at only half the couple
wishing a tottering couple on shaky ground
seeing a see–through couple pretending to be open minded
but with a closed relationship

Look! An impossibly traditional couple
Look! An impossible non–traditional couple
Oh the perils of coupitalism, couplism and coupledom
Will you join me in this next couple?
Sorry, I'm already coupled
Don't mess with the couples, please
Shuffle the couples on the block and see what happens

They're a subtle couple alright and so supple
They couple and uncouple every other week
Is that a straight couple? What an odd couple
Ever see an overnight couple staring into space or
a ridiculously happy couple caught in the act?
Couples are good for gossip, family dinners and the
Economy
Couple yourself and see
Young couples, couplets
Green couples, vegetarian

# ARE YOU HORNY?

Do you have a hard time communicating your sexual desires to others? Are you sometimes at a loss for words? Misunderstood? Embarrassed? Worry no more! Get to the point with our revolutionary new "Hi! Hi!" system. It's the fabulous, all–new inter–personal signaller that says: "Hi! I'm Horny!" With the amazing "Hi! Hi!" horn system you can let others know exactly how you feel and what you want. Whether it's your boyfriend, girlfriend, husband, wife, or that cute stranger from across the street, it's easy! Just pull out your "Hi! Hi!" horn signaller and squeeze: One honk means "Hi! I'm horny and available!" Two honks: "Are you interested?" And three: "Well golly gee, let's get together and do it!" No more confusion! No more illusions! Helps separate lust from love! Eliminates the need for corny pick–up rituals! Saves time! A real crowd pleaser! Great for single's bars! Ideal wedding gift! Don't delay! Get your "Hi! Hi!" horn system today! Available in three pocket–size models: Standard, Deluxe, and for the ultra horny, our Kenworth Diesel Blaster.

# LATE BREAKING NEWS

"We interrupt the final moments of the last period of this 7th and deciding game of the Stanley Cup Playoffs to bring you an important news bulletin: across North America tonight, women have taken control. The results: gangs of drunken, roving women are terrorizing men everywhere. Police are warning men not to go out alone at night.

Women are no longer listening to men.

Women are demanding that men shave their armpits and leg–hair or face public ridicule.

Women are demanding that men strip and show perfect pectorals before they can get a job.

Women are now earning more than men
for the same work.

Women are crowding men off bus seats and sidewalks.

Women are demanding that men with penises shorter than 12" undergo painful penis enlargement operations.

And finally, ladies and gentlemen, worst of all, women are peeing all over toilet seats and the floor.

More on this later. We now return to our coverage of the game."

# DOMESTIC WORKERS' BLUES

We're the brown women
you see in the park
blond children laughing
in our arms
We're the brown women
you see in the park
We're the Third World
in your living room

Seventy hour week
just work and sleep
no time off
what's a holiday?
Scrub and shine
washing floors all the time
Slaves had chains
we get the key
can let ourselves in and out
we're still not free

> "Polish that brass!"
> "Make that bed!"
> "Iron those dresses!"
> "Bake more bread!"
> "Deodorize the bowl!"
> "Buff the marble!"

Minimum wage?
Overtime pay? Ha!
Dream away girl
It's another 12 hour day

> "My Filipina's efficient,
> how about yours?"
> "Better than my Toyota,

*she doesn't rattle*
*on the curves!"*

Forced to live with the boss
on call night and day
We have no right to complain
it's the "Canadian way"
Love your kids
but miss our own

So far away
once was home
send them love and money
from the land of spilled
milk and honey
Now shoulder those mops
Aim those brooms
We're Filipina heroes
cleaning foreign rooms

*"Excuse me, ma'am*
*Can I have my pay?*
*I know you forgot again*
*What can I say?"*

( I won't ask twice
I'll forget to make dinner
If that doesn't work
I'll be sick all winter! )

For justice, for dignity
we've got each other
Filipina sister, daughter and mother

We're the brown women
you see in the park
blond children laughing
in our arms
We're the brown women
you see in the park
talking and organizing
We're the Third World —
rising
in your living room

# STRONG WOMEN

Strong women don't speak English
but wash floors, clean toilets
and sew jeans for the English

Strong women work nine to five,
five to one, one to nine
with or without pay
under one boss or two
with no time off
and the odd bum cheque

Strong women work silently
and sing softly
to themselves

Strong women sit together
on their way home in buses
on the subway
and smile to each other
knowing smiles

Strong women speak to the stars
about yesterday's dreams
and dreams to come
of the day they can dump the load
off their back
sweep the nagging boss
into the garbage
then go dance under the sun
with their children happy
running in fields full of daisies
sweet honeysuckle and laughing butterflies

Strong women wait
until everyone else is sleeping
before they weep

# SAM THE YARDER

He'd haul heavy—cut timber
down a rugged, steep slope
sitting in his "Yarder"
It was a hell of a big machine
like a giant giraffe with a 40 foot neck
and a cable
stretching from it's belly to it's chin
and way up the mountain
For 15 years Sam worked the gears
in that thing,
laughing, smiling, yarding

He'd work the side of a mountain
like you'd pick plums from a tree
reeling in his paycheque to feed his family
He'd hear a tooting horn,
another log to drag down
He knew all the signals, Sam
except the one that sent
a rockface
tumbling down

In Quatsino Sound
in beautiful BC
where mighty mountains
hold up the sky
and giant evergreens crash into the Pacific sea
where the rain never stops
and you work around the clock
there was a rumble and a roar
and Sam the Yarder,
worked no more

He's still down there
entombed in his Yarder
buried alive hundreds of feet under
All you can see poking through the tons, and tons of rubble
is Sam's line to the world:
a single steel cable, rusting in the rain
on the side of a mountain
that once echoed his name

# MAXWELL WASHED DISHES

Maxwell washed dishes
37 years worth
He could see them in his mind's eye
with leftovers still stuck to 'em
at least a million plates
all piled high teeterin' and greasy
touchin' the sky
He could see 'em, too
after the scalding hot water and soap
sparklin' clean, stacked so neatly
higher than any office tower
that's for sure
one hell of a pile
37 years worth
all washed at minimum wage
night after night
not one complaint
not a single broken dish
He could see 'em all
piled so precariously
And he could see himself
pulling off his rubber gloves
broad grin spreading
hands on his hips
something deep within him whispering
"Come on Maxwell, you can do it!"
giving that pile a little nudge
sending those dishes crashing down
on that god–damned
restaurant
And he'd hang up his apron
put on his hat
and walk home smiling

# WHITE FINGERS

There are men who deal in precious metals
from offices invisible to ordinary eyes
The only discomfort they ever suffer is running short
of ice and rye
They pick up the phone, swivel their chair,
dictate a letter or two
They run their powerful companies behind closed doors
pushing buttons, playing golf, pretending they never knew
No, they never heard of such a dreaded disease

*And we lost another man, another set of hands to "White Fingers"*

"Three thousand feet below the Earth
near the Quebec town of Chibougamau
in tunnels blacker than coal, that's right,
us miners descend with lunchbuckets and tools"

"Where no ray of sun has ever shone
We spend half our precious lives
We're two–legged moles who man dangerous machines
to feed our children and wives"

"We dig for copper, gold and lead
Drilling, boring, with machines
that rattle us from toes to head
Drilling, boring into the belly of the Earth
for ounces of metal that command more than they're worth
Down where night or day mean nothing at all
where no other living thing would ever go
where the only music you ever hear
is your teeth chattering with the chill
and the rhythm of the drill
You grip that drill, steady she goes
Your hands take the shock, the power just flows

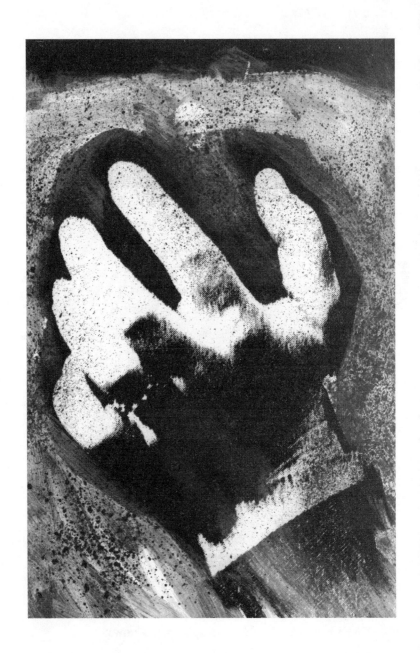

You know something's wrong, but you just can't quit
You try hard not to lose it
You grit your teeth and pray the job gets done
Then come the end of your shift, you rip off the gloves
and your fingers go numb"

*And we lost another man, another set of hands to "White Fingers"*

From Thetford Mines to Noranda and Chiapas
Miners complain at the end of each day
If it isn't the neck, the elbows or the wrists, it's
*"Honey, the doctor thinks it's lung cancer or bronchitis"*
And if it isn't the toxins, it's all the vibrations

  "We sell our hands to the Company
   They steal them from us and our family
   We dig the gold to decorate their fingers and necks
   They give us one of those fingers and a final pay cheque
   They'll always say it's our fault, we've suffered
   from this before
   Complain too much and they show us the door
   But when your fingers can't feel a baby's skin
   When you can't play your own accordion
   When your fingers turn as white as the snow falling

Where's the justice above ground or below
for a miner with *"White Fingers"*

# ANOTHER UNKNOWN SOLDIER

Who picks the fruit
cans the jams
cleans the fish
packs the hams
Who cleans the toilets
vacuums the floor
empties ashtrays
wipes off the door
Who digs the sewers
repairs the roads
returns home filthy
suffering heat and cold
Who can't find a room
a landlord to say yes
who can't afford schooling
is always fired first
Who does the work
others refuse
the dangerous jobs
that never make the news
Who takes the crap
ends up being used
sneered at, jailed
deported and ordered
to move
The unknown immigrant
That's who

# MAKE A DEAL WITH EL TIO

It's sugar cane liquor
in the early, early morn
but before you take a first swig
let a few drops fall
reverently
to the dirt floor at your feet
for El Tio

Some pray to the Virgin Mary
others stroke a lucky charm
but here in the highlands of Bolivia
in a mine so deep
you can never see the end
think before you speak
and thank El Tio

He owns this mine
and he owns all the wealth within
because "if God is in the sky
then El Tio is down below"
so ask no more
there's nothing else to know
just praise again El Tio

Out there he's cursed and scorned
he's evil they say he's a thorn
but in this mine down below
make your peace with him
and be happy it's done
or you won't make a dollar
from El Tio

Some say he wears a gold helmet
gold boots and a gold jacket
others swear he's yellow
made of sulphur so bright
with horns like a goat and a tail
but when you meet him you'll know
it's El Tio

Give him everything he needs
give him exactly what you use
invite him to join you at work
or at home
but remember:
strike it rich and you strike a deal
with El Tio

# IN THE JUNGLE

In the jungle by the river
beneath the shadow of the mountain
50 men worked like slaves to build a road

50 men dripping sweat, fighting heat
and the bite of snakes and flies and arrows flying
through the bush

> "My darling Anita,
>   the days are so long, the boss is a devil
>   singing the Company song
>   Don't worry about my health, I'm doing OK
>   but I miss you so much, day after day"

In the jungle by the river
beneath the shadow of the mountain
40 men slaved away to build a road

40 men who sold their souls
to the Company in the dark
desperate men who needed money right away

> "My darling Anita,
>   I hope you're well
>   Does the baby still cry when she hears the churchbell?
>   My body only aches with the pain of missing you
>   Your smile, your touch, I hope I'll see you soon"

In the jungle by the river
beneath the shadow of the mountain
30 men slaved away to build a road

30 men, muscles straining
eaten alive on their feet, felled by fever, falling faster
than the trees they cut

"My darling Anita,
  I see your face everywhere, I dream about you always
  I can smell your hair
  The work goes slow, don't worry I'm OK
  With the wages I'm making, we'll see a happier day"

In the jungle by the river
beneath the shadow of the mountain
20 men slaved away to build a road
20 men, tongues swollen, blisters bleeding
sores all broken
raw meat to treat the creatures of the night

"My darling Anita,
  I've lost track of the days
  The trees refuse steel but they eat our blades
  Your photo keeps me going when I'm worn and blue
  It's more than I can say for the lousy
  Company stew"

In the jungle by the river
beneath the shadow of the mountain
10 men worked like slaves to build a road

10 men under contract
"Finish the job, you signed the line
Not a penny to your family 'til you're through!"

"My darling Anita,
  I wish I'd never come
  How could I tell you sooner,
  this job will never be done
  Once we all drop dead, they'll hire another crew
  Because this road, this bloody road, they never told me
  it leads to Hell"

In the jungle by the river
beneath the shadow of the mountain
50 men had worked like slaves
to build a road, the road to Hell

50 men who didn't know
they'd never see their darlings again,
nor the money owed
50 men dying like flies
fighting heat and the bite of Company lies
that laid them all
yes each and every one of them
to rest

# ON GUARD FOR THEE

Canada
Province of Quebec

Notice concerning Article 178.23 of the Criminal Code of Canada

To: Mr. Norman Nawrocki

Sir,

     Following the provisions of Article 178.23 of the Criminal Code
(Canada's Law on the Protection of Privacy), I am informing you
that your private communications were the object of interception,
in accordance with judicial authority obtained for this purpose.
Signed,
(signature illegible)
specially mandated for the Quebec Solicitor General
(Rough translation of a registered letter received by NN)

NEWS ITEM: *"Spy Agency Obeying the Law, Watchdogs Say"*


I
When they visit you
late at night
you're never home
they never knock or
ring the bell or
leave a calling card
they walk in
through the locked door
silently
in the name of
"the true north strong and free"
according to the neighbours
they don't look like James Bond

II

When they listen in
on your phone calls
they never ask your permission
cough or participate
in the conversation
they just hear
what they want to hear
and forget the rest
it's none of their business
really
little men and women
with hunched shoulders and headphones
scratching themselves

III

When they place the bugs
in the kitchen, bedroom
and living–room walls
they never consult you
about the best spots
or rearrange the furniture
they match the paint beforehand
leave no traces
and call it another night's work
anticipating how much
free sex
this one's good for
thank Sony and the State
for the technology
they can almost taste
the orgasms

IV
When they read your mail
they never pencil in crude jokes
or stamp it
"opened for inspection"
they just copy the return address
and study the long distance hugs
kisses and ties that bind
the amount of truth confiding
the depth of fears and worries
spilling out all over their desk
someone gets to file "ex–lovers"
under "contacts national"
trust Canada Post
to deliver your letters
to caring, literate people
one with a degree
in psychology

V
When they follow your footsteps
they stay far enough behind
they never trip you or
throw snowballs your way
they're good
we've been told
they can spit on you
if they want
read the note over your shoulder
and you wouldn't really know
but sometimes something slips —
you're not alone today
useless people
walk your shadow

VI

When they park out front
far enough so you can't
smell them
(or so they think)
they never blast the radio or
make out in the front seat
they sit still
test wipers on rainless nights
slouch a bit look inconspicuous
and try to concentrate
on the faces that come and go
the excitement in your life
it's a boring job
it pays well
they can take turns sleeping
if they want


VII

When their late–model
two–tone beige car
cruises your alley
passenger door slightly ajar
the sun already set
they never burn rubber
huck beer bottles or honk
an arm reaches out — boing!
grabs your garbage bag full of
envelopes, peels and last nights
100 soggy kleenex
and hauls this in
another treat

for the dirty tricks boys
honest garbage men
couldn't do better

VIII
When they return home
each night tired
and crawl into their own beds
you wonder
if they realize that
"national security"
is such a big responsibility
not even they can do the job
properly
and that I,
ever–vigilant, freedom loving citizen
will therefore do my duty tonight
and keep an eye
on them

# BROTHER PETE

Uncle Ed had a Brother Pete
who died a lonely man
He was a farmer without wife or kids
but he left behind
$50,000 for Uncle Ed
Uncle Ed didn't have to think long or hard
He bought Brother Pete a
coffin fit for a king for
$25,000
a fancy wrought–iron fence for
the gravesite for
$11,000
a fine, engraved marble tombstone
polished just right for
$7,000
a priest who could deliver a
first class sermon with all the
trimmings, too, for only
$5,000
a three–piece measured to fit
wool suit for
$1,000
and a fresh, red rose for his
lapel for
$15.00
Uncle Ed said Brother Pete
worked hard all his life and
deserved it

# THE RAT KING

Son of a broken moon
Born on the third floor of the Sunrise
Abandoned in the garbage
Rescued by the rain
The beloved Rat King

> The Rat King lives in the bus shelter
> at the corner of Hastings and Main
> and shits in the bank
> The Rat King rips open doors
> to the City Jail to let the
> sunshine in and the prisoners out
> The Rat King blows fresh sea air
> into rooms where light bulbs swing
> and hot plates glow
> The Rat King snares bullets in his bare hands
> and smokes 'em on the courthouse steps

Raised in the shadow
of the scrawny green door
Wizened by the curve of a sucker punch
Smoother than the Mayor's shave
Smarter than a baseball bat
The beloved Rat King

> The Rat King brings pizza all–dressed
> with juicy roaches to the stately homes
> of slumlords
> The Rat King bowls with the balls of uptown Johns
> who jerk off without paying
> then tells their wives
> The Rat King takes politicians by their tongues
> and whirls them over his head
> into the City Dump

The Rat King sends gulls to lonely window sills
where old timers sit and wait

Denounced by the Pope
Blessed by the one–eyed crow
Blinded by the glare from a Cadillac's hubcap
Nursed in the palm of a Japanese blossom
The beloved Rat King

The Rat King ladles extra gravy onto the mashed potatoes
when the cook ain't lookin'
The Rat King makes the knives all silent
when they squabble and turn within
The Rat King gives an arm to the feeble,
a voice to the timid
a kick to those stuck in the muck
The Rat King walks barefoot on butts burning
and lets his people thru the turnstiles —
no charge
At night, the Rat King rests his head on a bench
and talks to the gods

Son of a broken moon
Born on the third floor of the Sunrise
Memorized by alley cats and weeds
Dead for a thousand years
The beloved Rat King

# OH CANADA!

Look here you great big Canadian flag
honking in the wind
I want to wipe my hairy ass with your freshness
your brazen nylon scrunching so proudly overhead
I want to wipe my hairy ass from bow to stern
with your red and white face
I want to highlight the wrinkles in that national conscience
I want to feel up close the look they call Canada
HONK! HONK!
The look directing hungry motorists, gas–starved vehicles,
potential new investors and children
all the way from the wilderness
to blessed ground to petro food stores
and to lonely outposts of engine trouble

Look here you great big Canadian flag
honking in the wind
accosting me across the broad back of this skinny land
Quit hanging on to that pole!
I want to cut you free
watch you climb heavenward out of sight —
an air–borne ball of tittering Canadiana

Just think! You could become a genuine home–sown UFO!
You could clog the intake of AIRFORCE I
and send it plummeting to the ground!
You could wreak havoc on the next formation of
Yankee super sky fighters en route to a foreign land
and send them back to Washington!

Be useful, eh
Make me salute you with pride with a bottle of home–brew
Say something memorable for school children to recite
in the dark years ahead when this land becomes another crooked
star, spent and spangled

listed on the market as a place where hosers
used to fly their colours to ward off un–American imperialists
Look here you great big Canadian flag
honking in the wind
Quit being a wimp! Attack while the scent is still fresh!
I guarantee Canada Geese will fly cover for you
Beaver coast–to–coast will fall power lines for you
Bear, moose and the last Canadian farmer will
redirect American troops crossing the border in pursuit of you
Go for it you great big Canadian flag!

Just think! A moment of glory brighter than the aurora borealis!
A moment of truth plainer than any goal Gretzky could score!
A moment of justice Ma Bell and Ma Liberty will never forget!

Look here you great big Canadian flag
honking in the wind
How many times did those Chinese seamstresses
curse you and the foreman
Reedeem yoursel!
And remember:
Once your glorious tattered pieces
flutter down back to cherished Canadian soil
hoards of vagabonds, under–bridge dwellers,
and dumpster picksters, will recycle your shredded weaves
into fancy underwear
fit for kings without flagpoles, subjects or shadows
Families across this vast land
will turn on the 6 o'clock news and rejoice
While the rest of us, inspired at last,
will dig out moth–balled Black Flags
to raise high as we take to the streets!

Look here you great big Canadian flag
Do it! Say good–bye and split!
You're spoiling my view

# AMERICACA

Good morning Americaca! This is CKIFR, Intelligence Free Radio, and I'm your host with the most for this misty morning, Bob Kaboom! Coming right up with sports, weather, traffic and all your favorite hits from Americaca hit men stationed around the globe protecting you and yours from them and theirs. And remember, listeners, if it ain't free, it ain't Americaca!

But first, here's a word from one of our freedom–lovin' sponsors, Coke: "Coke. You know it's the real thing when it comes all the way from the jungles of Bolivia in a CIA plane. Genuine, State–approved CIA coke. Snorters know it's the one. At your dealers now. Support the right to dictate. Snort it and watch your dollars finance another covert CIA operation. Available only in Americaca."

And now, the traffic report from our lovely, deodorized Donna:

"Yo, Bo! There's a steady flow of arms headin' north through Canader en route to Guatamaler, so border delays are expected. Meanwhile, planeloads of Americaca hostages coming back in trade from all around the world are clogging major air terminals. We advise commuters and tourists to stay home until all the boys and girls are back safely. Oh yea, that meltdown in the Pacific Northwest? It's causing havoc on the freeways. Do drive carefully. You'll get out quicker. That's it Bo!"

Thanks Donna! And remember: if it ain't safe, it ain't Americaca! Weather! That continuing radioactive drizzle will be light and won't bother those of you enjoying your vintage backyard bomb shelters – still on special, in lovely pastels, from this radio station for lucky survivors out there. Oh how we love you Americaca! Music! Here's our hit single from the El Salvadorean Police Academy Death Squad who recently toured Americaca to rave reviews everywhere!

"HEY! HEY! GET OUT OF OUR WAY! WE JUST CAME BACK
FROM THE USA!
HEY! HEY! GET OUT OF OUR WAY! NOW WE WORK FOR
THE CIA!!!"

And that's been #1 on our charts for weeks! Only in
Americaca!

Sports! Here's Ernie with a fast–breaking report from the
Mediterranean finals:

"Well, Bo, in the International Terrorist League, the US State
Department still maintains a healthy lead over its closest
competitors, outgunning, outbombing, outkilling everybody
in the first quarter. Seasons tickets for the best seats in our own
jumbo CKIFR helicopter gunship following all the action are
still available. That's it Bo! I gotta dodge some bullets now."

Thanks Ernie! Just goes to show you: we're still on top in
Americaca! And remember listeners: You don't have to be hit by
a flying brick or a molotov cocktail to realize you've got
problems. Call our own Mr. Fix It — Senator Oliver North —
on our trouble shootin' hot line. No global issue, no
neighbourhood menace is too hot for him to handle. You
can count on Ollie, just like you can count on the rest of us.
Because that's what it's all about in Americaca!

# 7-11 HEAVEN

You know, I had such a lousy day at work. The boss was on my case, the terminal was always screwing up, Sally wouldn't go out to lunch with me. It gave me a headache. So I got home, cracked open a couple of beer and just spaced out in front of the TV, not giving a hoot about anything other than how do I get out of here, how do I go somewhere far, far away.

And then I heard the voices. They were softly, sweetly, rising voices like the kind you hear in your sleep when you want to switch dreams. Those voices, softly, sweetly, rising voices that welcomed me, Arnold Schlafer, to "7–11 Heaven."

And there I was, little old Arnie in "7–11 Heaven," just like in a rock video, or even better, because this was no ordinary 7–11, no siree. And I'll bet none of the other guys at work had ever seen anything like it. This was a corner store from another world.

All that glaring neon, gone, replaced by soft lighting! There were no fish–eye security mirrors or cameras watching me! There were real plants everywhere! And the kids inside weren't screaming for popsicles! The checkout people didn't wear ugly uniforms but looked happy and healthy and had no acne! The woman behind the counter didn't scowl at me but actually smiled when she said:

"Welcome to 7–11 Heaven. We're open 24 hours a day and everything is free." I couldn't believe it! I rubbed my eyes and let out a "What the hell?"

"Don't worry, you're in the right place," she said. "Are you hungry? Just take what you need. You've worked. You've done your bit. Remember: from each according to their ability, to each according to their need. This is 7–11 Heaven."

"Wait a minute," I said. "I don't get it. 7–11 Heaven? Where's the boss. Let me talk to the manager."

"There are no bosses, no managers here," she replied.

"We're a worker–controlled, self–managed, food distribution outlet. No, no. Put your money away. How primitive. See, we have no cash register or credit card machine. There's no need to collect coloured pieces of paper from you. You just take what you need."

Now I was really confused and started to scratch and shake my head.

"Hey, hold on," I said. "If this is 7–11 Heaven, then where's all the junk food? You know, the Slurpees, the Twinkees, the Oreos, the Diet Cokes and the rows and rows of all that crap I can't live without. Like, where is it?"

"That's all history," she said laughing. "You'll find that stuff in the local museum, artifacts from a backward era. We stock only the finest in real food: fresh, organically grown fruit and vegetables, non–processed cheese, nuts and tofu. All the greens are from our own communal garden. This is 7–11 Heaven."

"But, but," I stammered, "Where are all the mindless video games, the stacks of National Enquirers?"

"All gone," she replied, "replaced by a lending library of books and educational videos about the Social Revolution and how the anarchists won."

"Cigarettes, please," I gasped, "Quick, I need a smoke. Give me a pack of cigarettes."

"Gone, too," she said. "Here, have a stick of natural licorice root and suck on it instead. You're in 7–11 Heaven now. Relax."

"But I can't live without junk food, without money, without, AAAGH!" I screamed. "Get me outta here!"

I awoke in a cold sweat, the nightmare over, my alarm clock ringing in another work morning. Last night's TV was now blaring aerobics. I rubbed my sleepy eyes. It was the dawn of a new day. I needed some mouthwash and a shave.

# DRINK IT, DOW!

*News stories about the multi-national Dow Chemical Company's "leaks" of toxic wastes into the St–Clair River in Ontario, Canada, appear with alarming regularity. The reports are nearly always followed by company reassurances that "there's no danger to the public" despite the conflicting evidence from other sources.*

You take another leak
in a local river
your bladder bursting with a bitter brew
and you poison it with
your industrial piss
then you've got the nerve
the corporate gall
the corporate balls to say
      "There's no danger to the public"?
Drink it, DOW, Drink it

You take your leak in a convenient spot
you point your prick in the mouth of St–Clair,
captive
she can't get away
run somewhere else
so you gush long and hard
and her screams are silent gurgling waters
no one can hear
you've done it again, DOW

You've pissed out of American planes
a fiery death straight from the hell of your
Michigan boardroom
Napalm — the jelly bomb
They couldn't scrape it off
their burning skin
the Vietnamin
so they died
remember:

"DOW shall not kill"
Now, DOW, you're pumping out hell
like toxic dioxins
from "blobs" in the river to itchy skin
when do we burn from
drinking it in and
     "There's no danger to the public"?
Drink it, DOW, Drink it

You poison this planet with
your corporate dick and
when the public cries you
just zipper it in 'til it
springs right out again
dripping and pissing DOW
out of my tap into my glass
your corporate slime, your corporate line
and the State turns a
blind eye oh yes

One of these days you'll
take your last leak
in the middle of the night when you sneak out back
we're gonna jump you fucker
bend you in two and
shove your prick so
red white and blue
right back into you and
watch you piss
There'll be no danger to the public
once you
Drink it, DOW, Drink it
to the very last drop

# TANK FUCKING

Imagine a tank
refusing to fight
making love, not war
engaging the enemy in an amorous embrace
locked together
on fields of battle
fucking tanks
fucking the armies
and fucking the war

Imagine the tanks
joyful and gay
fucking each other instead of the people
telling their officers to fuck themselves
10 ton deserters
discarding their armour and shells

Imagine the tanks
confounding historians
refusing to defend profits or kings
rolling across borders in search of new lovers
and nights on the town
French tanks, French ticklers, just fooling around

Imagine these tanks
converted to Peace
muzzles all rubbered
protecting the world from fatal diseases
like the State, Imperialism and War
thinking tanks, responsible tanks
united in condemnation
Thank goodness tanks fuck

# THE NASTIEST BREWERY
# IN THE WEST...

It was one of those mean summer days
when your feet baked in your boots
and the sun rode your back like a
merciless bronco buster. I needed a drink.
I walked into a bar and ordered a beer.
Then I noticed the grizzled old timer in the corner
giving me and my drink the eye. There was something
about that man. I invited him to join me and he did, a rye
in one hand and a glint in his eye.

   "You're new in these parts, eh stranger?" he growled.
   I nodded.
   "Well before you taste that beer, let me tell you a story
      about the nastiest brewery in the West.."

When the West was still wild back in 1873
Adolph Joseph Coors tamed it with his brewery
the largest in the world in Golden Colorado
loomed over the town like a giant fortress you know

Some said Coors brewed a great–tasting beer
bottled in a plant with a racially pure atmosphere
by an all–American German business pioneer
who hated having any non–white folk near
Coors, red–blooded, Christian and proud

The Coors started by keeping their brewery colour–free
and later became America's most notorious dynasty
It wasn't enough just to guard their plant's purity
they engaged in ultra–right wing philanthropy

Coors, a brewery where the Ku Klux Klan
were welcomed to meet and drink
with the family congregation
It wasn't 'til the 1960s and the civil rights fight
that Coors racist hiring fell under the spotlight
Coors would urge workers to oppose the Civil Rights Act
warned blacks would replace whites if the Act became fact

Mexican–Americans hot under Coors' collar
started a strike protesting Coors colour bar
they boycotted the brew
the supremacists withdrew — a little
then pumped millions into buying a Coors image all new

But not before they donated a helicopter
to Denver cops, to patrol Chicano barrios and terrorize
black neighbourhood blocks

The smoldering '70s Coors tried to resist
fighting birth control, the women's movement
it was all "Communist"
They co–founded the Heritage Foundation,
financed this blight
an anti–abortion, anti–ERA, anti–gay brain of the ultra–right
You see, Coors tried to control their workers' morality
Step out of line or the closet at the brewery
and Coors would use their heavy artillery
vowing to dismiss anyone
    "who violates the common decency of the community"
      and thus "catch queers if they got past the lie detector test"

Call 'em vicious, call 'em slime
Coors was America's sophisticated
anti–gay front line
    *"Put AIDs victims in leper colonies under quarantine"*
    *"Make death penalties for lesbians and gays our*
      *national routine"*
Queer bashing, Coors style

Coors never really stopped their hateful discrimination
so they got boycotted, bombed and boycotted again
The AFL–CIO, the New World Liberation Front,
community groups by the dozens
dented their sales by 30%, a cool $30 million
Still Coors kept steering their bucks into
repression like the right–wing think tanks
cranking out their ammunition

All this before the reign
of Coors crony, Ronald Reagan
advised by the Coors Heritage Foundation
on how to reduce the deficit and assert American might:
    *"Scrap workplace health and safety codes*
    *Abolish the minimum wage*
    *Cut social services; send racist regimes aid*
    *Funding for the handicapped is counter-productive*
    *Develop space-laser weaponry*
    *"Morally objectionable" music's subversive*
    *Beef up internal security"*
By May 1982 Reagan and his administration
had implemented 61% of the Right recommendations

While Coors financed fundamentalist terror at home
down in Nicaragua bloodthirsty Contras roamed

mutilating, torturing, raping and killing
terrorizing a people resolute and unwilling to support 'em
But Uncle Sam's proxy army was fighting a losing war
and lost a major battle in 1984
when Congress derailed Reagan's gun gravy train
No dice, no money for the Contra campaign —
or so they said
Poor Contras, with two years of action
and 10,000 victims to date
there they were, an army without a State
sitting 'round torched villages with empty dinner plates
Who could save their holy mission?

In stepped Coors and the World Anti–Communist League
willing to help moneyless international gunslingers in need
Coors rang the chow bell in the American corporate mess
and raised an easy million a month
to ease the Contras distress
Coors, Contra sugar daddy, patron saint and saviour
the single largest American private donor
Suds money from the family
that knows
what's best
to silence Godless, subversive peasant unrest

They brought Contras to America
to ride the campaign trail
to show fellow fascists how their donations didn't fail
and what they got for their investment:
red hands, keeping the world as pure as a Coors beer

"And that," said the old–timer, "is only the tip
of an ugly iceberg." I tipped my hat to the guy, left the beer
untouched and walked out to join the Coors boycott.

# WARSAW: A BAR MELECZNY

"Oh Poland"
one knife is all it takes
to slit a throat
or stick between two skinny ribs
but here in downtown Warsaw
the Bar Meleczny has no more knives
and so we butter our buns
with grimy fingers
Janocek had a hatchet
Jarozelwski had martial law
Solidarnosc had thousands of steel mills,
docks, factories, offices and farms
waiting for the word to strike
and they did
now they don't
and so the Bar Meleczny has no more knives
But, the cooks
keep cleavers sharpened and ready
to cut through the fat
that slowly begins to pad
the new bosses, like the old bosses
the new smiles on old faces
the new excuses and
the old "excuse me, I thought you understood?"
and the soup lines get longer
and the zlotys stop here
and the hunger in the eyes
drives the knives
through the sighs of
"Oh Poland"

# THE MAGON BROTHERS

They say down in Mexico,
on a moonless night when
coyotes wail into the void and owls
give the signal,
the Magon Brothers will ride high across
that desert sky
lassooed to the brightest
shooting star

They say the Magon Brothers
armed with guns 'n typewriters,
books and bullets
will drop into the saddles
of two great white horses
and lead a column of the poor
north from the jungles of Chiapas
to the factories along the Rio Grande
all shouting
*Tierra Y Libertad!*

They say this mighty column
bristling with dangerous ideas
and powerful dreams
travelling on foot and bicycle,
in beat up old buses and Chevys
will take back all the land
from the privileged
and kick 'em out

They say no laws will be tough enough
to scare them
No army strong enough to stop them
No TV lies loud enough to drown out their cries
of *Tierra Y Libertad!*

They say the Magon Brothers,
Ricardo and Enrique, started folk
thinking a long time ago
when they declared
all wealth should be shared
all men and women free
all governments abolished
replaced by a new, more just world
of Anarchy

They say you'll know when
the Magon Brothers ride again
In the mile high cloud of dust, smoke and ashes
you'll see 'em
In the thunderous pounding of heartbeats, hooves
and drums, you'll hear them
In the aftermath of the storm that follows
wherever they go, you'll know
Tierra Y Libertad!

# EIGHTEEN TONS

18 tons
11,600 gallons
Northern Type
CNR steam locomotive
#6167
at least 45 feet long
shiny and black as night
with wheels as tall as a man
massive cast iron beauty beast
built to outlast
empires, presidents and bank machines
now parked
beside the Guelph
city bus depot
on 100 feet of rail
behind a wire fence
while a rabbit
hops in and out
of its shadow

# HERE ARE THE POEMS

There are poems that were written
  before the birth of the bullet
  poems that pierced armour and
  rattled brains and buried their way
  through mountains so high

There are poems that were written
  to hold up walls, fill in holes,
  be swept away by tides and winds, burned
  by the sun into ice and ancient stone,
  poems so feathery they could fly by themselves
  into distant homes and silently enter the
  dreamworld of Mother or Child, Soldier or
  Peasant, Thief or Hangman

There are poems, hard–edged poems
  that can slice swiftly through the darkness
  and leave a drop of blood on satin sheets white
  spoiled forever

There are poems written for feasts and famine,
  for the blind and the bold, the near and the far,
  poems written because someone must not keep the
  world waiting nor refuse the offer of a word or
  two from an unmeasurable distance
  If no one writes them where will they go?
  Who will they visit?
  Where can they rest?

There are poems that were written
  without sleep or pen or paper or
  hour of day to mark them without
  peace of mind or permission or the
  voice of Authority or a marketing executive

to modulate their pitch or their trajectory
to determine their worth or stamp them with
a rotten tomato for public consumption

There are poems that were written
    because radar–defying weapons were
    needed to blast holes into the Pentagon,
    the Kremlin and Parliament
    to explain Life on Death Row
    to shut out the clanging of steel doors in
    a Tennessee women's prison

There are poems that were written
    because panhandlers and collectors of
    aluminum cans never gathered enough pennies
    to melt into red hot spears

There are poems that were written
    to gather friends and family, strangers and
    dead souls to grab hands and spirits with the force
    of a deep yearning
    for a greater sum of the parts
    for the love gone missing

There are poems that were written
    to help light a fire in the middle of a park
    in the middle of the night
    to draw instruments of music near
    so that the dance of poetry
    could begin

And there are poems that were written
    simply because

# ACKNOWLEDGEMENTS

Thanks to Peter Bailey, the original "New Life Poet" who shared his poetry and a vision with me so long ago; to Lizzy Sara May (1918 — 1990), dear Dutch friend & writer who said "write!"; to Fortner Anderson who kept pushing; to Rachel Melas for her sense of words & music; to my family who were always there, and to all the anarchists, dreamers & Zapatistas of the world for their presence.

And a very special thanks to Don Stewart & Cindy Oakley for their much appreciated editorial assistance; to Harl Thomas & Minda Bernstein for introducing me to the 21st century; to spud & katiemur for their indispensible artistic & typographical talent, skill & enthusiasm; to Ramsey Kanaan for his indefatigable publishing spirit; to Sylvain Côté, musical wizard, dear buddy & partner in RA; & to David Lester for his friendship and brilliant graphics. May a rebel moon shine brightly for all of you!

# Rhythm Activism DISCOGRAPHY

Rhythm *Activism* — cassette, March '86,
Les Pages Noires 001 Montréal
Rhythm *Activism* "Live" — cass. with 16 page booklet, Feb '87, LPN 002
*Resist Much – Obey Little* — cass. with 16 pg booklet, Dec '87, LPN 003
*Louis Riel In China* — cassette, Sept '88, LPN 004
*Un Logement Pour Une Chanson* — cassette, Feb '90, LPN 005
*Fight the Hike!* — cassette, March '90 LPN 006
*Perogies, Pasta and Liberty* — cassette, April '90, LPN 007
*Oka* — cassette, Sept. '90, LPN 008
*War is the Health of the State* — cassette, Jan. '91, LPN 009
*Oka II* — cassette, April '92, LPN 010
*Tumbleweed* — cassette, Feb. '93, LPN 011
*Blood & Mud* — CD, Nov. '94, LPN 013C / Konkurrel K158c,
Amsterdam / cassette, Nikt Nie Nie Wie, Nowy Targ, Poland
*More Kick!* — CD, Nov. '95, LPN 014C / Konkurrel, Amsterdam
*Buffalo, Burgers & Beer* — cassette, Dec '95, LPN 015

## VIDEOS

*Alive & Kicking* — a 10 year retrospective documentary of RA, Dec
'95, LPN 016V, Montréal
*That's The Way We Tie Our Shoes* (C'est comme ça qu'on attache nos souliers),
RA live on tour in Europe, April '96, Unbend Films, Amsterdam

## Norman Nawrocki solo:

*I Don't Understand Women!* — cass, 1993, LPN012 (excerpts from an
anti-sexist "sex" comedy cabaret)

RA CDs distributed in Canada by Festival Records; in Europe by
Konkurrent; in the USA by AK Distribution. Or, direct from:
LES PAGES NOIRES,
P.O. Box 891 Station Desjardins,
Montréal, Québec H5B 1B9
email: rhythm@nothingness.org

Rhythm Activism website:
http://www.nothingness.org/music/rhythm/

# COLOPHON

*Rebel Moon* is set in Hermes and Joanna and was designed by katiemur of Dada Typographics for an edition published by AK Press of Edinburgh, London, and San Francisco.

I COULDN'T PAINT GOLDEN ANGELS: SIXTY YEARS OF COMMONPLACE LIFE AND ANARCHIST AGITATION by Albert Meltzer. ISBN 1-873176 93 7; 400pp, two color cover, perfect bound 210 x 245 mm; £12.95/$19.95. Albert Meltzer (1920-1996) had been involved actively in class struggles since the age of 15; exceptionally for his generation in having been a convinced Anarchist from the start, without any family background in such activity. I Couldn't Paint Golden Angels is a lively, witty account of what he claimed would have been the commonplace life of a

**I COULDN'T PAINT GOLDEN ANGELS**
BY
**ALBERT MELTZER**

worker but for the fact that he spent sixty years in anarchist activism. As a result it is a unique recounting of many struggles otherwise distorted or unrecorded, including the history of the contemporary development of anarchism in Britain and other countries where he was involved, notably Spain.

His story tells of many struggles, including for the first time, the Anglo-Spanish co-operation in the post-War anti-Franco resistance and provides interesting sidelights on, amongst others, the printers' and miners' strikes, fighting Blackshirts and the battle of Cable Street, the so-called Angry Brigade activities, the Anarchist Black Cross, the Cairo Mutiny and wartime German anti-Nazi resistance, the New Left of the 60s, the rise of squatting — and through individuals as varied as Kenyata, Emma Goldman, George Orwell, Guy Aldred and Frank Ridley — all of which have crowded out not only his story, but his life too.

*"If I can't have a revolution, what is there to dance about?"* — *Albert Meltzer*

ANARCHISM: ARGUMENTS FOR AND AGAINST by Albert Meltzer. ISBN 1-873176 19-8; 80pp, two color cover, perfect bound 5-1/2 x 8-1/2; £3.50/$5.00. Everything you wanted to know about anarchism, but were afraid to ask. A new revised and updated edition of the definitive pocket primer on anarchism.

From the historical background, and justification of anarchism, to the class struggle, organization, and the role of an anarchist in an authoritarian society, this slim volume walks the reader through the salient points, theory and practice, of this much misunderstood and misaligned phi-

losophy. From workers self-defence to the myth of taxation, the second half of the book runs through the gamut of objections and queries, from Marxist-Leninists, liberal-democrats, fascists, and the average person. If you're wishing you were better informed, or just mildly curious, this is the place to start.

REINVENTING ANARCHY, AGAIN edited by Howard J. Ehrlich. ISBN 1-873176 88-0; 400pp, two color cover, perfect bound 6x9; £13.95/$19.95. A fully revised and updated printing of this seminal work of contemporary anarchism, theory and practice, the first edition of which sold over 20,000 copies. Reinventing Anarchy, Again brings together the major currents of social anarchist theory in a collection of some of the most important writers from the United States, Canada, England and Australia.

Organized in eight sections, the book opens with an exploration of the past and future possibilities of anarchism, then moves to consider the "necessity" of the state and bureaucratic organization as well as the meaning of the "anarchist contract." The third of the theoretical sections tackles the hard questions for social anarchists confronting the foundations of libertarian socialist and liberal democratic thought. In part four, the contributors traverse the defining characteristics of the various feminisms moving to a concrete statement about the nature of anarchafeminism. In the fifth section about work, the authors consider the issues of worker's self-management, resistance through the underground economy, as well as the implications of the abolition of work itself. In the final three sections, the anthology addresses the culture of anarchy, self-liberation, and the process for building an anarchist society. The book ends with a set of trenchant observations on the current scene by the editor.

Howard J. Ehrlich is the editor of *Social Anarchism*, the premier English-language magazine of anarchist writing. Trained as a sociologist and social psychologist, Ehrlich directs The Prejudice Institute, a national policy research and educational organization studying group prejudice and ethnoviolence in all of its manifestations. He brings a unique blend of social science, anarchist theorizing and community action to this anthology.

To Remember Spain: The Anarchist And Syndicalist Revolution Of 1936 by Murray Bookchin; ISBN 1 873176 87 2; 80pp two color cover, perfect bound 5-1/2 x 8-1/2; £4.50/$6.00. In these essays, Bookchin places the Spanish Anarchist and anarchosyndicalist movements of the 1930s in the context of the revolutionary workers' movements of the pre-World War II era. These articles describe, analyze, and evaluate the last of the great proletarian revolutions of the past two centuries. They form indispensable supplements to Bookchin's larger 1977 history, *The Spanish Anarchists: The Heroic Years, 1868–1936* (to be reprinted by AK Press). Read together, these  works constitute a highly informative and theoretically significant assessment of the anarchist and anarchosyndicalist movements in Spain. They are invaluable for any reader concerned with the place of the Spanish Revolution in history and with the accomplishments, insights, and failings of the anarchosyndicalist movement.

# NEW BOOKS FROM AK PRESS

THE STRUGGLE AGAINST THE STATE AND OTHER ESSAYS by Nestor Makhno, translated by Alexandre Skirda; ISBN 1-873176-78-3; 128 pp, two color cover, perfect bound 5-1/2 x 8-1/2; $9.95/£7.95. Born of peasant stock in Gwlyog-Polye, Ukraine, Nestor Makhno became an anarchist after the Russian Revolution of 1905. Sentenced to death for armed struggle, his sentence was commuted to life imprisonment. Liberated in 1917, he organized an army of anarchist resistance against both the Bolsheviks and the White counterrevolutionaries. Throughout his period of struggle, he consistently advocated the creation of anarchist communism in the most difficult and impractical of conditions. Forced to flee by the Bolsheviks, he eventually ended up in exile in Paris. Marginalized

and impoverished, in poor health as a result of wounds sustained in fighting against the Whites and the Bolsheviks, and time spent in prisons inside tsarist Russia before the Revolution and in Eastern European prisons en route to exile afterwards, Nestor Makhno wrote occasional essays in self-vindication and in vindication of the peasant insurgent movement that bore his name. Published primarily for fellow-exiles, these essays ranged from the theoretical and analytical, establishing him plainly as a deliberate as well as a visceral anarchist, to challenges thrown out to his enemies — including some Jewish anarchists — to produce proof of the alleged anti-Semitism of his movement in revolutionary Ukraine. Makhno was determined that the next time anarchism, acting in the light of experiences dearly bought, revamped and more disciplined thanks to its Organizational Platform, might reap the rewards proportionate with the commitment and sacrifice of its activists. The essays in this volume date from his period in exile.

SCUM MANIFESTO by Valerie Solanas. ISBN 1-873176 44-9; 64 pp, two color cover, perfect bound 5-1/2 x 8-1/2; £3.50/$5.00. This is the definitive edition of the SCUM Manifesto with an afterword detailing the life and death of Valerie Solanas. "Life in this society being, at best, an utter bore and no aspect of society being at all relevant to women, there remains to civic-minded, responsible, thrill-seeking females only to overthrow the government, eliminate the money system, institute complete automation and destroy the male sex. . . . On the shooting of Andy Warhol: I consider that a moral act. And I consider it immoral that I missed. I should have done target practice."
—Valerie Solanas

## FRIENDS OF AK PRESS

In the last 12 months, AK Press has published around 15 new titles. In the next 12 months we should be able to publish roughly the same, including new work by Murray Bookchin, CRASS, Daniel Guerin, Noam Chomsky, Jello Biafra, Stewart Home, new audio work from Noam Chomsky, plus more. However, not only are we financially constrained as to what (and how much) we can publish, we already have a huge backlog of excellent material we would like to publish sooner, rather than later. If we had the money, we could easily publish 30 titles in the coming 12 months.

Projects currently being worked on include previously unpublished early anarchist writings by Victor Serge; more work from Noam Chomsky, Murray Bookchin and Stewart Home; Raoul Vaneigem on the surrealists; a new anthology of computer hacking and hacker culture; a short history of British Fascism; the collected writings of Guy Aldred; a new anthology of cutting edge radical fiction and poetry; new work from Freddie Baer; an updated reprint of The Floodgates of Anarchy; the autobiography and political writings of former Black Panther and class war prisoner Lorenzo Kom'boa Ervin, and much, much more. As well as working on the new AK Press Audio series, we are also working to set up a new pamphlet series, both to reprint long neglected classics and to present new material in a cheap, accessible format.

Friends of AK Press is a way in which you can directly help us try to realize many more such projects, much faster. Friends pay a minimum of $15/£10 per month into our AK Press account. All moneys received go directly into our publishing. In return, Friends receive (for the duration of their membership), automatically, as and when they appear, one copy free of every new AK Press title. Secondly, they are also entitled to 10 percent discount on everything featured in the current AK Distribution mail-order catalog (upwards of 3,000 titles), on any and every order. Friends, if they wish, can be acknowledged as a Friend in all new AK Press titles.

To find out more on how to contribute to Friends of AK Press, and for a Friends order form, please do write to:

| AK Press | AK Press |
|---|---|
| PO Box 40682 | P.O. Box 12766 |
| San Francisco, CA | Edinburgh, Scotland |
| 94140-0682 | EH8 9YE |

# Some Recent Titles from AK Press

Social Anarchism Or Lifestyle Anarchism: An Unbridgeable Chasm by Murray Bookchin. ISBN 1 873176 83 X; 96pp two color cover, perfect bound 5-1/2 x 8-1/2; £5.95/$7.95. This book asks — and tries to answer — several basic questions that affect all Leftists today. Will anarchism remain a revolutionary social movement or become a chic boutique lifestyle subculture? Will its primary goals be the complete transformation of a hierarchical, class, and irrational society into a libertarian communist one? Or will it become an ideology focused on personal well-being, spiritual redemption, and self-realization within the existing society? This small book, tightly reasoned and documented, should be of interest to all radicals in the "postmodern age," for whom the Left seems in hopeless disarray. Includes the essay *The Left That Was.*

Ecofascism: Lessons from the German Experience by Janet Biehl and Peter Staudenmaier. ISBN 1 873176 73 2; 80pp, two color cover, perfect bound 5-1/2 x 8-1/2; £5.00/$7.00. Includes two essays, "Fascist Ideology: The Green Wing of the Nazi Party and its Historial Anatecedents" and "Ecology and the Modernization of Fascism in the German Ultra-Right," along with an introduction.

Which Way for the Ecology Movement by Murray Bookchin. ISBN 1 873176 26 0; 80pp two color cover, perfect bound 5-1/2 x 8-1/2; £4.50/$6.00. Bookchin calls for a critical social standpoint that transcends both "biocentrism" and "eco-centrism"; for a new politics and ethics of complementarity, in which people, fighting for a free, nonhierarchical, and cooperative society, being to play a creative role in natural evolution. He attacks the misanthropic notions that the environmental crisis is caused mainly by overpopulation or humanity's genetic makeup and resolutely points to the social and economic causes as the problem the environmental movement must deal with.

The Realization and Suppression of the Situationist International: An Annotated Bibliography 1972-1992 by Simon Ford. ISBN 1-873176-82-1; 149pp two color cover, perfect bound; £7.95/$11.95. This annotated bibliography contains over 600 references that chart its rise to fame from obscurity to celebrity. More than a bibliography it is the most substantial reference book yet produced on the group and provides a gateway to the related worlds of underground publishing, anarchism, and the contemporary avant-garde. There are also two sections solely devoted to documenting the little known British and American "pro-sit" scenes.

Immediatism by Hakim Bey. ISBN 1 873176 42 2; 64 pp four color cover, perfect bound 5-1/2 x 8-1/2; £4.50/$7.00. A new stunning collection of essays from the author of Temporary Autonomous Zone, beautifully illustrated by Freddie Baer.

*AK Press publishes and distributes a wide variety of radical literature. For our latest catalog featuring these and several thousand other titles, please send a large self-addressed, stamped envelope to:*

AK Press
PO Box 40682
San Francisco, CA
94140-0682

AK Press
P.O. Box 12766
Edinburgh, Scotland
EH8 9YE